Ra Wee Book A' Book A' Glesca Banter

by Iain Gray

Lang**Syne**

PUBLISHING

WRITING *to* REMEMBER

LangSyne

PUBLISHING

WRITING *to* REMEMBER

79 Main Street, Newtongrange,
Midlothian EH22 4NA
Tel: 0131 344 0414   Fax: 0845 075 6085
E-mail: info@lang-syne.co.uk
www.langsyneshop.co.uk

Design by Dorothy Meikle
Printed by Printwell Ltd
© Lang Syne Publishers Ltd 2019

ISBN 978-1-85217-447-7

Ra Wee Book A' Glesca Banter

Inspired by Robin J Hyland
A Glasgow lad o' pairts

Born and raised in Glasgow's very own Drumchapel, fondly known as 'The Drum', I am completely familiar with the Glesca banter. Throughout my career in retail I have travelled all over Britain and encountered some great dialect and people. None of them however warmed, pleased and cheered me as much as when I heard my own native tongue.

I hope you enjoy this collection of words and sayings, as much as I do reading and hearing them.

Robin J Hyland
Bookseller & Accordionist

From the old variety halls to the theatre stage and the television screen, generations of Glasgow comedians have thrilled audiences through their hilarious exploitation of the city's unique banter.

FOREWORD

It was in October of 2009 that a rather curious job advertisement appeared in a Scottish newspaper:

"Glaswegian" interpreters. Translation company seeks speakers of Glaswegian English with knowledge of vocabulary, accent, nuances, to meet interpreting needs of clients who find it an unexpected challenge.

Placed by the London based company Today Translation and aimed at finding a translator who could help foreign visitors to the city whose 'business English' fell significantly short of enabling them to comprehend the local dialect, the advertisement attracted close on 500 applicants.

It was announced in February of the following year that Jonathan Downie, originally from Glasgow, better and more fondly known by its proud citizens as *Glesca*, had been selected for the unusual post.

A languages expert with a degree in translation and conference interpreting from Scotland's Heriot

Watt University, the 26-year-old became the world's first official interpreter of Glaswegian.

About a year previous to his appointment, the city's First Glasgow bus company launched an initiative to teach Glaswegian to its sizeable number of drivers of Eastern European, mainly Polish, origin.

Veteran bus driver James Lillis, who had plied the city's bus routes for 30 years, was engaged by the company to head up the initiative, which involved him learning basic Polish to allow him to pass on his knowledge of Glaswegian to the drivers.

The scheme has proved such a success that, in recognition of his efforts, Mr Lillis was presented with an award for lifelong learning from the Scottish Government.

The Today Translation and First Glasgow initiatives highlight the extent to which Glaswegian is recognised as very much a language in its own right – very often completely baffling in its complexity to outsiders.

Popularly known as the banter, the lingo, or the patter (more properly *Ra Banter, Ra Lingo, Ra Patter*), it comprises the everyday words and sayings that are considered unique to Glasgow and its environs – although some everyday words, such as *wean* (small child), are also in common usage throughout the length and breadth of Scotland.

The roots of Glasgow banter lie in the dim and very distant past when, in about the fourth century AD, Germanic dialects came to British shores through the influx of Angles, Jutes and Saxons.

These dialects became known as Old English, later developing into Middle English.

It was a form of this Middle English, infused with a distinctive Northumbrian dialect, that became the most common form of the language of the Scots.

Further unravelling what is a veritable linguistic tangle, the Middle English that forms the basis of Scots is sub-divided into distinctive groupings that include Central Scots, Southern Scots, Northern Scots, Island Scots and the Highland English of the Highlands and Western Isles.

Also distinctive to Scotland, of course, is the lyrical language of Gaelic, which has enjoyed a resurgence in recent years not only in Scotland but also in her fellow Celtic neighbour of Ireland.

The Glasgow banter is a rich and highly colourful blend of aspects of all of the above, with the important addition to the mix of the 'Irish English' imported to Glasgow and its environs by the large numbers of

Irish who settled there, particularly throughout the nineteenth century.

It also owes much to the everyday lives and experiences of the tenement-dwelling Glasgow working class, in particular the former Clyde shipyard workers and others involved in heavy engineering.

For the vast majority, Glasgow once represented a particularly harsh environment in which to survive, dogged by poverty and ill health – and this is reflected to this day in the markedly self-deprecating and self-compensating humorous banter of Glaswegians.

Glaswegians are not readily impressed by the pretensions of others, particularly those with an over-inflated opinion of themselves, and this is also reflected in the banter.

The city has also always had an unfortunate relationship with alcohol and its unfortunate effects and, as our A to Z shows, this is highlighted by the number of words and phrases related to alcohol and states of inebriation – such as *steamin* and *stoshus*.

One unfortunate sign of the times is the appearance in the Glesca Banter in recent years of words and sayings related to drugs and their effects.

The influence of drugs, in common, it has to be

said, with other major cities, is so prevalent that no A to Z of the banter could choose to ignore it.

The banter has many unique aspects, incomprehensible to outsiders until they manage to attune themselves to them.

These include the substitution of 'a' or 'i' for 'of', as in *a pint a milk*, rather than *a pint of milk*, while many words and phrases are run together and delivered at almost machine-gun speed.

One example of this is *arrabacka*, for *at the back of*, while other examples came to the attention of a wider public in the 1970s through Glasgow-born actor and comedian Stanley Baxter's *Parliamo Glasgow* television sketches.

A spoof on the *Parliamo Italiano* programme, *Parliamo Glasgow* featured Baxter as a language coach explaining phrases such as *Izzata marra oan yer barra, Clara?/Is that a marrow on your barrow, Clara?* and *Gies a punna burra furra murra/Give me a pound of butter for my mother*.

In addition to *Parliamo Glasgow*, the banter also memorably featured in the repartee of the late actors and comedians Jack Milroy and Rikki Fulton, as *Francie and Josie*.

It was *Francie and Josie* who, on both stage and

television, popularised what is now the common *Hawraw rerr!* For *Hello, there!* and *stoater*, to describe an attractive young lady.

In more recent times, not only the Glasgow banter in particular but also the banter of Scots in general, has been enriched by words and sayings from popular Scottish television comedies, such as *Rab C. Nesbitt*, *Chewin' the Fat* and *Still Game*.

It is from *Chewin' the Fat*, for example, in sketches played by Ford Kiernan and Greg Hemphill, that *Gonnae no dae that!* was popularised – a phrase that now adorns a range of merchandise including T-shirts and mugs.

The Glesca Banter is constantly being added to and evolving, recent additions, for example, being the use of fond nicknames for well-known Glasgow landmarks such as *Lally's Palais* – Glasgow's Royal Concert Hall and referring to former Lord Provost Pat Lally – and the *Squinty Bridge*, the Glasgow Arc Bridge that crosses the Clyde at a distinctive angle.

Another common phrase to be found in *Ra Wee Book A' Glesca Banter* is *Pure Dead Brilliant*, to describe something particularly good, or satisfying – and it was as *Pure Dead Brilliant* that in February of

2011 Japanese people learning to speak English rated the highly distinctive Glasgow accent.

In a survey carried out by Northumbria University, it was found that Glaswegians, at least according to Japanese ears, have the most attractive accent, related to a range of personality traits, in the English speaking world.

Pure Dead Brilliant, indeed …

A is for...

A/Ah Used before a noun as a substitute for 'of'. As in *Ah had a bowl a porridge for my breakfast*. Similar to 'i'/'ih' and 'o'/'oh'

Aboot About. As in *Whit wiz that all aboot?/What was that all about?*

Actin' it Playing up or exaggerating a particular situation. As in *He's really actin' it*.

Aff Off. *As in Ah'm aff tae my bed/I'm off to my bed*.

Afore Before. As in *Ah'll have a wee swally afore ah huv ma dinner/I'll have a small libation before I have my dinner*.

Affrontit Embarrassed. Similar to 'black affrontit'.

Ah I.

Ah'd I had. As in *Ah'd a good time last night*.

Aheid Ahead. As in *The shops are jist aheid i us/ The shops are just ahead of us*.

Ah'll I will. As in *Ah'll call you later*.

Ah'm I'm. As in *Ah'm going out tonight*.

Ah'mur I am. Similar to 'ah'm.'

Ah'murny I am not. As in *Ah'murny going out tonight*.

Ah've I have. As in *Ah've goat ti go oot the night/ I have to go out this evening*.

Ain One, or own. As in *This is my ain book*.

Airm Arm.

Alane Alone. As in *Leave me alane*.

Alang Along.

Alky An alcoholic.

Alwiz Always. As in *I will alwiz love ye, doll!/I will always have great affection for you, my lovely lady!*

An And.

Anaw Also/in addition to. As in *I'll have a pint of beer and a packet of crisps anaw*.

Anither Another. As in *I'll have anither packet of crisps*.

Anoll And also.

An that And all the rest. As in *I just went oot ti buy some bread and milk an that/I merely went* *out to buy some bread and milk and sundry other articles.* Similar to 'anoll'.

Aroon Around. As in *What goes aroon comes aroon.*

Arra An arrow or 'all the' or 'at the'.

Arrabacka At the back of. As in *The cheese is arrabacka the fridge.*

Arrabest/orrabest All the best. A common farewell to a friend.

At it Similar to 'actin' it. As in *He's really at it this time.*

Auld Old, used in an affectionate manner to describe an old relative, friend or old person in general.

Auld jin/auld yin Old one, viz. an old person. As in *I suppose we better visit the auld yin this weekend/I suppose we should visit our elderly relative this weekend.*

Aw/awe All. As in *Who stole aw the pies?*

Awa Away. As in the popular terse injunctions *Awa an bile yer heid!/Away and boil your head!* and *Awa ye go, ya mug ye!/Away you go, you mug you!*

Awfy Awful. As in *Ah've an awfy sore heid*/*I have a terrible headache*.

Awright Alright. As in *Ur you share you're feelin awright? Are you sure you are not feeling ill?*/ *Is something troubling you?*

■B■ is for...

Ba/Baw A ball. As in *The ba's oan the slates*/ *The enterprise we are engaged in unfortunately has to end because of circumstances beyond our control*.

Babby Baby.

Baccy Tobacco.

Bachle A person of less than average height, usually a female.

Baffies/buffies Slippers.

Bahookie Backside. As in *I tripped up and landed on my bahookie*.

Balloon An idiot with an over-inflated sense of his/her intelligence.

Baltic Extremely cold. As in *It's pure baltic today*.

Bampot One of many Glaswegian terms for someone who is intellectually challenged.

Bamstick Similar to 'bampot'.

Banjo To hit.

Banjoed Having been hit. As in *I banjoed him after he called me a bampot*.

Banter Everyday words and sayings, as in the everyday banter unique to Glaswegians. Similar to 'lingo' and 'patter'.

Barney A row or a fight. As in *There was a real barney in the pub last night*.

Barra A barrow.

Barras, The Famous market in the east end of the city, also affectionately known as *Ra (the) Barras*.

Bar L Barlinnie Prison, in the east end of the city.

Bauchle A worn out item of footwear.

Bead rattler A Roman Catholic.

Beamer A red face caused by acute embarrassment.

Beauty/Ya Something very pleasing, giving great satisfaction. Also see 'Ya Dancer'.

Beelin Very angry. As in *I was pure beelin/I was very angry*.

Beezer Anything that is very pleasing or satisfying. As in *I had a pure beezer of a time oan my holidays/I had a very good time while on holiday*.

Bell tinky To devote your greatest effort to a task. As in *Gie it bell tinky/Give it your all*.

Belter/Beltur Similar to 'beezer'.

Ben Behind.

Berries, The Similar to 'beezer' and 'belter'. As in *That dinner was joost the berries/The dinner was very satisfying, it really hit the mark*.

Big Hoose Barlinnie Prison, in the east end of the city.

Big Man Someone considered of above average height for a Glaswegian. Also a friendly greeting to someone whose name you don't know. *As in Hello, big man, could you tell me the time?*

Big Yin Similar to 'Big Man', but can also refer to someone who has achieved success and fame through a particular pursuit, for example the

Glasgow actor and comedian Billy Connolly, fondly known as *The Big Yin*.

Bile Boil.

Billy Boy A supporter of Rangers Football Club or someone of the Protestant faith in general.

Binchi/Binchy A bench.

Bingo bus A police van.

Bin Howker Someone who scavenges from rubbish bins. Similar to 'midgie raker'.

Black affronted Very embarrassed. As in *The wind blew my skirt up – I was black affronted*.

Black neck A dirty person. Someone whose personal hygiene leaves a lot to be desired.

Blaw Blow. Also slang for cannabis, hash.

Blawin fur tugs Blowing for tugs. Out of breath after strenuous activity. *As in I wiz blawin fur tugs after walking up that steep hill/I was out of breath after walking up the steep hill*.

Blootered Very drunk. *As in I got really blootered at Hogmanay*.

Bleach To beat up.

Blue Nose Similar to 'Billy Boy'.

Boak Vomit, or to vomit, usually with reference to something unpleasant. As in *It wid gie ye the boak/It is so bad it could make you vomit*.

Boatle Bottle.

Boatle a soup Bottle of soup. Refers to the highly popular and potent Buckfast tonic wine.

Boax A box or to box. See 'Xboax'.

Bob Hope Rhyming slang for 'dope' such as cannabis/hash.

Boggin Dirty or smelly.

Bolt To run away, or to eat quickly.

Boost Steal.

Bottle it To withdraw from a course of action, or a fight, because of fear.

Bottle merchant A coward.

Bottling An old Glasgow ritual where a young woman about to be married would be paraded through the streets by her friends and young men were invited to gift her a small sum of money, in return for a kiss from the bride-to-be; derives from the 'bottles' of alcohol the bride-to-be and her friends would carry.

Boozer/Boozers A public house or someone with a particular fondness for alcohol.

Boudo Money.

Boufin Similar to 'boggin'. As in *You're feet are pure boufin/You're feet are emitting a particularly noxious odour*. Also a general term for something not considered particularly good. As in *I went to the pictures last night, but the film was boufin*.

Bountie/Bounty Bound to, certain to. As in *He's bountie have a hangover tomorrow after drinking all that whisky*.

Braw Beautiful or very good.

Breid Bread.

Buckfast Commando A regular imbiber of Buckfast (see 'boatle a soup').

Buckfast Triangle The Lanarkshire areas of Airdrie, Bellshill and Coatbridge reputed to have a large number of Buckfast devotees.

Buckfast Valley The Lower Clyde Valley.

Buckie Buckfast tonic wine.

Budgies The peculiar Glasgow fashion statement of wearing one's socks (usually white sports

socks) over the top of one's tracksuit bottoms.
See 'trackies'.

Bunty A victim of bullying.

Burd/Burds Birds. Young women.

Burra Butter. As in the famous Stanley Baxter
Parliamo Glasgow sketch *Gies a punna burra
furra murra/Give me a pound of butter for my
mother.*

But Commonly used at the end of a statement as a
form of emphasis. *As in I might look daft, but
I'm not daft, but.*

Buzzin Feeling the effects of alcohol or drugs.

Byjingo The game of bingo. As in *I hope I get a
win at the byjingo tonight.*

Byraway By the way. Similar to 'but'. As in
I refuse to pay for that, byraway.

C is for...

Caird Card. As in *He's a caird-carrying member
of the Monster Raving Loony Party.*

Cairpet Carpet.

Cannae Can't. As in *I cannae dae that/I can't do that*.

Cargo Alcohol. As in *He's carrying a fair cargo/He has imbibed a great deal of alcohol*.

Cargo shop Anywhere that sells alcoholic beverages.

Cauld Cold.

Caur Car.

Cawed Called. As in *Whit's she cawed?/What is her name?*

Chanty Chamber pot.

Charge/Charged Drunk.

Charred Drunk. *As in I was well charred last night*.

Chavvy Someone from outwith the Glasgow area.

Cheeba Hash.

Cheeky water Alcohol.

Chib To slash with a knife or razor.

Chibbed Slashed.

Chippie/Chippy Fish and chip shop.

China Friend/pal.

Chong Hash.

Chuckies Pebbles or stones.

Claes Clothes.

Claim/Claimed To single someone out whom you want to fight (for whatever reason). As in *You're claimed, pal!*

Clatty Dirty and untidy. As in *Her hoose is really clatty/Her house is a mess*. Similar to 'boggin', 'boufin', 'honkin', 'manky', 'mawkit', 'mingin'.

Clippy The conductor/conductress who would 'clip' your ticket on a bus or, particularly, the former Glasgow trams.

Clockwork Orange Glasgow's Underground (subway) transport system whose original carriages were painted a distinctive orange.

Close The ground floor passageway of a tenement building.

Cludgie Lavatory.

Clype/Clyped To tell on, 'grass up'. As in *I sneaked oot tae the pub last night, and ma pal clyped oan me tae my wife/I sneaked out to the public house last night for a few drinks and my* *friend later grassed me up by telling my wife all about it*.

C'moan Come on! As in the memorable phrase used by the former Glasgow clippies (see clippy) to hasten up the departure of their passengers from the bus/tram – *C'moan, get aff!*/*Come on now, hurry along and disembark*.

Comfy Come from. As in *I comfy Glesca*/*I come from Glasgow*.

Connie A candle.

Cooncil Council. Specifically Glasgow City Council.

Cooncil juice Ordinary tap water.

Corpy Name for the former Glasgow Corporation (now City Council) and still commonly used.

Couldnae Couldn't. As in *Ah couldnae care less*.

Coup/Cowp To fall over, or a place where rubbish is dumped, or a description of a very untidy place. As in *Her hoose is a real coup*.

Coupon The face. As in *Whit's wrong wi yer coupon?*/*Why are you looking so miserable?*

Creashie Overweight.

D is for...

Da Dad/father.

Dabbity A sticker or tattoo.

Dale A diving board. Thought to derive from 'deal', the type of wood originally used for diving boards.

Dancer/Ya Something very pleasing, giving great satisfaction. As in *I had a big win oan the hoarses. Ya dancer!/I placed a winning bet on the horse race and won a great deal of money. I'm very pleased!* Similar to Ya Beauty!

Dancin/The Dancing. As in *I met a burd at the dancin/I met a young lady at the dance*. Glasgow was at one time renowned for its dance venues, particularly *The Plaza* and *The Barrowland Ballroom*.

Daud/Dod/Dodda An amount, or dollop, of. As in *Gies a wee dodda burra oan ma totties/Give me a small amount of butter on my potatoes*.

Dead/Deid Very much. Notably *Pure Deid (Dead) Brilliant*. As in *I think Lady Gaga's new* *record is pure dead brilliant.* Also *Pure Dead Amazin/Pure Dead Cool.*

Deafie/Sling a deafie Similar to 'dingy'. Ignoring what someone has said or requested by pretending not to hear. As in *He slung me a deafie/He pretended not to hear.*

Dial To slash someone on the face with a knife or razor.

Diddy An idiot. As in *He's a real diddy!*

Dime bar Total dimwit.

Dingy To ignore. As in *Ah asked him tae dae the washing up and he joost gave me a dingy/I asked him to do the washing up, but he simply ignored me.*

Dinnae Don't. *As in Dinnae dae that/Don't do that.*

Dizzy The act of failing to turn up for a pre-arranged meeting. To stand someone up. As in *He wiz supposed to meet me ootside the pub, but gave me a dizzy.*

Dog/Dogged To play truant. As in *My pal dogged school yesterday.*

Doin A beating up. As in *He gave him a real doin/He severely beat him up.*

Doll　Affectionate term used by males for their better half. Particularly popular in recent times through the Glaswegian television comedy character *Rab C. Nesbitt* with reference to his wife, *Mary Doll*.

Doon　Down. Notably found in *Doon the Watter*, the old Glasgow holiday pastime of taking a trip down the river Clyde on a paddle steamer such as the Waverley, proudly the world's last sea going paddle steamer.

Doughball/Dough heid　Someone of decidedly limited intelligence.

Drap/Drapped/Drappy　Drop, dropping, drop of. As in *Gies a wee drappy water in my whisky*.

Dreep/Dreepin/Dreepy　To drop, or hang from, as in the children's game of dreepin from a wall.

Dobber　Dimwit.

Drookit　Soaking wet. As in *Ah'm totally drookit after being caught in the rain*.

Drum/The　Drumchapel area of the city.

Dunted　Mildly inebriated. Or having been hit.

E is for...

Eachy peachy/Eeksy peeksy A draw, or equal shares.

Easturhoose The Easterhouse area of Glasgow.

Eat the breid A glutton. As in *Quick, hide the grub, here comes eat the breid*.

Edge/Edgie Keep a lookout for you're pals while they are engaged in some nefarious activity.

Edinburger Derogatory term for a citizen of the rival city of Edinburgh.

Eejit Idiot. As in *Look at yon eejit/Look at that idiot*. Also a common Irish term, from which the word derives.

Eekies Equals. A debt that has been settled. As in *Here's the money you lent me. We're now eekies*.

Efter After, afterwords, later. As in *Ah'll see you efter/I'll see you later*.

Efternin Afternoon.

Elba Elbow. As in *She's given me the elba/ She has ended our relationship*.

Electric soup Alcohol.

Embra Edinburgh.

Emdy Anybody/Anyone. As in *Did emdy else see that?*

Erra/Ers/Errsa There's/There's a. As in *Errsa train coming now*.

◤F is for...

Face A selection of choice Glaswegian terms for those unfortunates whose facial looks leave much to be desired:

Face like a camel eatin' sherbet.

Face like a chewed caramel.

Face like a bag a (of) spanners.

Face like a bulldog chewing a wasp.

Face like a burst couch.

Face like a burst tomato.

Face like a dug lickin' pish (urine) aff (off) a nettle.

Face like a Halloween tumshie (turnip).

Face like a melted wellie (rubber boot).

Face like a welder's binchi (bench).

Face like a well skelped (struck) backside.

Face that looks like he/she has been dookin (ducking) fur (for) apples in a chip pan.

Face that looks like he/she has been set oan (on) fire and put oot (out) wi (with) a golf shoe.

Fae/Frae From. As in *He's fae Edinburgh.*

Faither Father.

Fandan Idiot.

Ferr Fair. As in the annual two-week holiday known as the *Glasgow Ferr/Glasgow Fair.*

Flaky/Throw a flaky A sudden mad turn. Take a mad turn.

Fleein/Fleeing High on alcohol or drugs.

Flurt To flirt.

Foalian Following. As in *Please stop foalian me aboot/Please refrain from following me about.*

Frankie Vaughn's Rhyming slang for the hands, or *hauns/hawns. As in Get yer Frankie Vaughn's intae the sink and wash the dishes.*

Fu/Ful Full, usually of alcohol.

Ful eh it Full of it, either alcohol or self-importance.

Furrit Forward. As in *Ah started work on this hours ago, but I'm still nae further furrit/I started work on this hours ago, but I'm still no further forward*.

G is for...

Gallus Very confident, brass necked, fearless.

Gaun Go/Go on.

Gaun yersel Go yourself. Go on as you are, you are doing very well.

Geeza/Gies Give me. As in *Gies a brekk/Give me a break* and *Gies peace*.

Geggie Mouth. As in *Shut your geggie/Please refrain from speaking, you are annoying me*.

Gemm/Gemmy Game, as in football, or game as in bold or up for it.

Ginger Any type of carbonated soft drink.

Glasgoed Very drunk.

Glasgow briefcase A plastic bag, also known as a 'poly', (polythene) bag.

Glasgow oyster Cheap and common culinary delicacy of a meat pie inside a roll.

Glasgow salad Chips/French fries.

Glass cheque An empty bottle, such as a ginger or a beer bottle, from which you can claim a small cash sum when you return it.

Glesca/Glesga The proud city of Glasgow.

Glesca kiss A head butt.

Goat Got. As in *I goat a new pair of shoes*.

Gonnae Going to. As in *Gonnae no dae that/Please refrain from what you are doing, I'm finding it intensely annoying*.

Gowpin Hurting. As in *Ma feet ur gowpin wi all that walking. Ah cannae wait tae take ma shoes aff an put oan ma baffies/My feet are really sore after all the walking I have done. I can't wait to take off my shoes and put on my slippers*.

Greetin Crying.

Greetin faced Constantly moaning and complaining.

Gub/gubbin Mouth or to hit. As in *Shut yer gob* or *I gave him a real gubbin*.

Gundies Underpants. Similar to 'scants'.

Gupty Go up to. As in *Gupty the bedroom and bring me doon ma baffies/Go up the bedroom and bring me down my slippers.*

■ is for...

Hackit Ugly.

Hairy A rather rough and ready young Glasgow girl, as in *She's a real wee hairy.*

Hale Whole.

Hampden roar Score. Rhyming slang that refers to Hampden Park, Scotland's national football stadium on the south side of Glasgow. Refers not only to football scores, as in *Whit's the Hampden roar?/What's the latest, what's happening, what are you up to?*

Haud Hold. As in *Haud yer wheesht/Please be quiet.*

Haudy Hold of. As in *Keep a haudy yer haun bag/Keep hold of your handbag.*

Hauf/Half Usually a measure of whisky, as in *Gies a wee hauf/Give me a small whisky.*

Haufers Halfers. As in *Let's go haufers on that meal/Let's share the bill equally*.

Haufwit Halfwit.

Haun/Hauns/Hawn/Hawns Hand/hands. As in *Gies a wee haun wi this/Give me a little hand with this*. Similar to 'Frankie Vaughn's. Also *Keep yer haun oan yer happeny/Keep your hand on your halfpenny*. Common advice given to a Glasgow girl, normally from her mother, to retain her maidenly virtue when stepping out with a young man.

Hauner A hand. To give someone a hand, to help them out.

Haw Hey!

Hawraw Hello.

Hawrawrerr Hello there. A common Glaswegian greeting made famous by the late comic duo Francie and Josie, who would welcome their audiences with *Hawrawrerr, chinas* (friends).

Heavy bongoed Heavily under the influence of drugs.

Heavy scran A big meal.

Hee-haw Nothing. As in *I've got absolutely hee-haw in the bank*.

Heid Head.

Heidbanger Headbanger. A very disturbed, and disturbing, person.

Heid the baw A bighead.

Hen Familiar term for a girl.

Hielanman's Umbrella Highlandman's Umbrella. A section of the city's Argyle Street that is sheltered from the elements by a railway bridge running overhead.

Himshie A woman who looks like a man.

Hingin Hanging.

Hingoot A woman of questionable sexual morals. One who doesn't 'Keep a haun on her happeny'.

Hoachin In great abundance. As in *The river is hoachin' with fish*.

Hoaladays Holidays. As in *Ah'm off oan ma hoaladays tae Majorca/I'm off on my holidays to Majorca*.

Honkin Dirty or smelly. Similar to 'boggin' and 'boufin'.

Huckle To lift, arrest. As in *He was huckled by the polis/He was taken away by the police*.

Hudgie A lift. Usually one child carrying another on his/her back.

Hun A supporter of Glasgow Rangers Football Club.

Hunner One hundred. As in *Ah need a lenna £100/I need a loan of £100*.

Huv/Huz Have/has.

Huvnae/Huznae Have not/has not. As in *I huvnaue goat £100 to gie you a lenna/I haven't got £100 to loan you*.

■ is for...

Icey An ice cream van.

Ih/i Of. Similar to 'a'/'ah' and 'o'/'oh'.

Int/Isnae Is not.

Intae Into.

Intae it Into it. As in *Get intae it/Let's go for it/Get stuck in*.

Ither Other. As in *See what's on the ither TV channels/This programme we are watching is rubbish. See if you can find anything better*.

Izzat/Izzata Is that/Is that a. As in the Stanley Baxter *Parliamo Glasgow* sketch *Izzata marra oan yer barra, Clara?/Is that a marrow on your barrow, Clara?*

◢ is for...

Jaggy Prickly.

Jags/The Partick Thistle Football Club.

Jaiket Jacket.

Jaikey An alcoholic.

Jake Cheap alcohol, usually cheap cider.

Jaked Drunk.

Jay A hash joint.

Jaxie Backside Similar to 'bahoukie'. As in *I*

tripped and landed oan ma jaxie/I tripped and landed on my backside.

Jeeked Exhausted. As in *I'm totally jeeked after walking all the way back from the bingo.*

Jeely Jelly or jam. As in *jeely piece/jam sandwich.*

Jen up Honest, genuinely. *As in I saw a UFO last night, jen up!*

Jile/jiled Jail/jailed As in *Joe has been jiled.*

Jimmy How Glaswegians address male strangers. As in *Hello there, Jimmy.* Also as a form of warning to someone not to overstep the mark, as in *See you, Jimmy!*

Jin One. Similar to 'yin'.

Jine Join.

Jined Joined. As in *Tam has jined the Army.*

Jinkies The best. As in *Joost the jinkies/Just the best.*

Joab Job. As in *Joe has lost his joab.*

Joost Just.

Jouk To avoid.

◼️**K** is for...

KB'd Knocked out – either through exhaustion, drink or drugs.

Keeker A black eye.

Keelie Term used by outsiders for a Glasgow man. As in *Glesca keelie*.

Keep the heid Act calmy. As in *Don't panic, joost keep the heid*.

Kerry Carry. As in *Gies a haun tae kerry ma messages/Give me a hand to carry my shopping*.

Kerry oot A carry out. A supply of alcohol bought for a party or for normal home consumption.

Keys A truce, or the act of surrendering. As in *Ok, keys! Let's call it quits* or *I give in*.

Kin Can.

Kindae Kind of. As in *It's kindae cold in here*.

Kinna Can I? As in *Kinna buy you a drink?*

Kinni Cannot.

■ is for...

Lady Godiva Rhyming slang for a 'fiver', £5.

Laldy Great effort. As in *Gie it laldy/Give it you're full effort*.

Lally's Palais A fond term for Glasgow's prestigious Royal Concert Hall, in the city centre, eventually established through the dogged perseverance of former Lord Provost Pat Lally.

Lamp To hit.

Lamped Having been hit.

Lang Long.

Lavvy Lavatory.

Lecky Electricity.

Len Loan.

Lenna/Lennie a Loan of. As in *Gies a lennie a fiver/Give me a loan of £5*.

Lingo Everyday words and sayings, as in the everyday lingo unique to Glasgow. Similar to 'banter' and 'patter'.

Loupin Jumping, full, very busy. As in *The dancin was loupin last night*. Similar to 'hoachin.'

Lumber A male or female partner. As in *I went tae the dancin last night and got a lumber*.

M is for...

Ma/Maw/Mither My, as in *Ma hoose/My house* or mother.

Mackie/Macky To hit with a stick.

Mad wi it Mad with it. Usually through the consumption of a great deal of alcohol.

Maddy A mad turn or a violent fit of bad temper. As in *She took a real maddy*.

Mah My. As in *Mah heid is burstin!/I have a splitting headache* or *I just can't cope with all this, it's too much!*

Mair More.

Malky To assault by head butting or with a knife or razor. Similar to 'Glasgow kiss'.

Manky Very dirty. Similar to 'clatty', 'boggin', 'boufin', 'honkin', 'mingin', 'mawkit'.

Masell Myself.

Mawkit As 'manky', above.

Menchy Graffiti.

Messages Shopping, usually for basic items such as bread and milk. As in *Ah'm aff tae get the messages/I'm off to the shops*.

Mibbe/Mibby Maybe. As in *Mibby ah wull, mibby ah wulnae/Maybe I will, maybe I won't*.

Midden A rubbish heap or a general term for something dirty and untidy. As in *Her hoose is like a midden/Her home is a real mess*.

Midgie A rubbish bin.

Midgie man Council worker who collects and empties the bins.

Midgie raker Someone who scavenges from bins. Similar to 'bin howker'.

Mince Absolute rubbish or nonsense. As in *Yer talking mince!/You are talking rubbish*.

Mincie heid Someone whose head is full of nonsense.

Mind To remember or to watch out. As in *Mind to*

set the alarm clock tonight or *Mind you don't slip on that ice*.

Mindin A gift or present. As in *It's their wedding next month. Ah'll huv tae get them a wee mindin/I'll have to get them a small present*.

Mingin Very smelly. Similar to 'boggin' etc.

Mintit Very well off financially. As in *He's pure minted, so he is*.

Miroculus Insensible through drink.

Moolurd Totally inebriated. Similar to 'miroculus', 'steamin', 'stoshus' etc.

Morra/Ramorra Tomorrow.

Motur Motor, car.

Munter An ugly woman.

Munter hunter Someone who chases after ugly women.

Murder polis! Murder police! A cry of alarm. Also *Help, murder polis!*

◼ is for...

Nae No. As in *Nae bother/That would be no trouble at all* or *You don't have to thank me, it was no problem at all.*

Nae Kiddin No kidding. Similar to 'jen up'.

Naebdy Nobody, no-one. As in *There's naebdy in.*

Nane None.

Napper The head.

Naw No.

Ned Abbreviation of Non Educated Delinquent. A common term for a young male prone to criminal behaviour.

Neebur/Neeburs Neighbour/neighbours. As in *The new neeburs have moved in.*

Nineteen canteen An undetermined date. As in *Ah cannae remember when it happened. It was back in nineteen canteen or something/I can't remember when the event I'm referring to occurred. It was some time in the past.*

Nip To have sexual congress with or to annoy by nagging. As in *She's nippin ma heid aff/She's really annoying me with her incessant nagging.*

Noo Now.

Nugget Idiot.

Nuhin Nothing. As in *There's nuhin happening*.

Numpty Yet another term for an idiot.

Nyaff/Wee nyaff An annoying person, usually of small stature.

O is for...

Oan On. As in *He's oan the bus*.

Oany Any. As in *Do you have oany cash oan you?*

Offy Off licence premises where one can purchase alcohol.

Oh/o Of. Similar to 'ah' and 'ih'.

Offski/Fur the offski Off, leave, leaving. As in *Ah'm fur the offski/I'm leaving now*.

Old Firm The rival Glasgow football teams Rangers and Celtic.

Oor Our. As in Scotland's well-loved comic character *Oor Wullie/Our William*.

Oot Out. As in *Oot yer face/Extremely drunk*.

Ootsider Outsider.

Ower Over. As in *The party's ower*.

◗ is for...

Pad aboot Walk about, usually in an aimless manner.

Paddy's Market A famous and former cheap outdoor market in the Saltmarket area of the city.

Paddy wagon Police van.

Paisley screwdriver A hammer. A derogatory term used by Glasgow tradesmen in relation to their Paisley counterparts who, in turn, return the insult by describing a hammer as a Glasgow screwdriver.

Pal A common way in which to address a stranger. As in *Excuse me, pal, could you give me a light?*

Pan breid Rhyming slang for pan bread and meaning decidedly deid, or dead.

Pap Put out. As in *Pap that in the bin*.

Papped Thrown out, thrown over, rejected. As in *Ah've papped my boyfriend*.

Paradise Fond nickname used by Celtic Football Club fans for Celtic Park, their stadium in the east end of the city.

Pat and Mick Sick. As in *He's oan the Pat and Mick/He's off work because of illness*.

Patter Everyday words and sayings, as in the everyday patter unique to Glasgow. Similar to 'banter' and 'lingo'.

Pearl diver Rhyming slang for a 'fiver', £5.

Peely wally Looking off colour.

Peg To have sexual congress with.

Pelters A great deal of, or strenuous effort. As in *Gie it pelters!*

Perr Pair.

Perra Pair of. As in *I bought a new perra shoes*.

Pertick The Partick area of Glasgow. Also see 'The Jags'.

Piece A sandwich.

Pish pundit A bookmaker/bookie.

Plug To stab.

Poke A paper bag or to have sexual congress with.

Pokey hat An ice cream cornet.

Pokka Bag of. As in *pokka chips*.

Polis Police.

Polomint City New Town of East Kilbride, so nicknamed because of its high number of roundabouts.

Puggy Fruit machine.

Punky A lift. As in *Gies a punky up the sterrs/Carry me up the stairs*.

Pure Extremely. As in *Pure dead brilliant!*

Q is for...

Quality Anything of a satisfyingly high standard, something that gives great satisfaction, something that meets with your approval.

Quality Men Young Glasgow men, usually happily inebriated or under the influence of drugs, who use 'quality' as part of their everyday vocabulary. As in *Ah went to see that new Brad Pitt movie aboot the zombies, World War Z, an that wiz filmed in Glesca. Ah goat a joab as an extra cos they didnae need tae gie me any make-up or claes an ah joost hud tae turn up as ah wiz. It's pure quality, man!/I have seen the new Brad Pitt movie about the zombies, World War Z, which was filmed in Glasgow. I was hired as an extra because the film production company did not have to spend money on giving me make-up or clothes. I just had to turn up for filming as I was. It's absolutely brilliant, my friend!*

Quoted Held in very high regard.

▉ is for...

Ra The. As in *Ra street/The street*.

Ragin Very angry or severe. As in *Ah've a ragin toothache/I have extremely painful toothache*.

Rammy A row. Similar to 'stushie'.

Randan An exciting and dissolute time. As in *I wiz*

oot oan the randan last night/I had a very good time last night, I hope my wife doesn't find out.

Rank Very smelly. Similar to 'boggin', 'boufin', 'mingin' etc.

Rank rotten Very bad, well beneath standard. As in *That meal was rank rotten*.

Rat That. As in *See rat ower there/Look at that over there*.

Redd To tidy or prepare. As in *Reddy up* or *Redd the table for dinner*.

Red scud Cheap and nasty red wine.

Reddy/Reedy/Big Reddy A face flushed red with embarrassment. As in *She's got a big reddy*.

Reekin Smelling badly. As in 'boggin', 'boufin', 'mingin', 'rank' etc.

Rerr Rare.

Rerr Terr Rare tear. A grand old time or a very enjoyable activity.

Riddy Ready. As in *Are you riddy yet?*

Rinoo At the present moment. As in *It's happening rinoo*.

Rip yer knittin oot Untangle your knitting. As in *It wid rip yer knittin oot/It would fill you with complete and total despair*.

Rocket A mentally unbalanced person.

Rubber ear To ignore what someone is saying. As in *I asked him to put the dinner on, but he just gave me the rubber ear*. Similar to 'deefie' and 'dingy'.

Rubbered Heavily under the influence of drugs.

Rubbery gub Rubber mouth. A chatterbox, usually someone who speaks out of turn.

S is for...

Sair Sore. As in *I've got a sair heid/I have a sore head*.

Sangwidge A sandwich.

Sannies Plimsolls or a sandwich.

Sanoffy It's an awful. As in *Sanoffy pity he's loast his joab/It's an awful pity he has lost his job*.

Sarry Heid/The The Saracen's Head, Glasgow's oldest public house, in the east end of the city.

Scadge A tramp or a mixture of tobacco and hash used to make a joint.

Scaff Scruffy.

Scaffie Street sweeper.

Scants Underpants. Similar to 'gundies'.

Scoobies The police.

Scooby A clue. Rhyming slang derived from the television cartoon character Scooby Doo. As in *I huvnae a scoobie/I don't have a clue*.

Scran Food.

Scratcher Bed. As in *I'm aff tae ma scratcher/I'm off to bed*.

Scud To hit, or state of nakedness, or very cheap and nasty wine or cider.

Scud book A dirty magazine.

Scunner A nuisance. As in *He's nothing but a wee scunner*.

Scunnered Extremely fed up. As in *Ah'm really scunnered with all this bad weather*.

Scunt To strike.

Scunted Having been struck.

Share Sure. As in *Are you share?/Are you sure?*

Sheep it Run away, usually from an altercation.

Shooder Shoulder or to shake.

Shoot the craw Shoot the crow. To leave, depart. As in *That's nearly midnight, I'll huv tae shoot the craw/That's nearly midnight, I'll have to leave for home*.

Shoppie Shop.

Skank Emitting a noxious odour. Similar to 'boggin' etc.

Skite To strike mildly.

Smidgeon A very small amount. As in *Just put a smidgeon of sugar in my tea*. Similar to 'toaty'.

Sminkin/Sminky Yet another term, similar to 'boufin' etc., indicating dirty, smelly.

Sneck To kiss.

Snecking The act of kissing. As in *I saw them snecking in the close last night*.

Snib To detain – normally to confine an offspring to his/her home as punishment for a misdemeanour. As in *No, you can't go out to* *play with your pals. You're snibbed for the rest of the week!* Also *The Snib/Prison.*

Spam Valley The affluent suburbs of Bearsden and Milngavie.

Speshul Special.

Sponny Lucky. As in *She was very sponny at the bingo last night.*

Square go A one-on-one fight. As in *Right, you, Ah'm challenging you to a square go!*

Squinty Bridge Nickname for the Clyde Arc Bridge, noted for how it crosses the river at an angle.

Stank A drain.

Stank monster A particularly ugly person.

Stappit Stuffed.

Stappit fu Stuffed full. As in *Ah'm stappit fu after eating that fish supper.*

Staun Stand. As in *I'll staun you a drink.*

Steaky A knife.

Steamie/The A public facility for washing clothes that was very popular before washing machines became more affordable. Also the name of a very popular play written by Glasgow's very own Tony Roper.

Steamin/Steamboats Very drunk.

Sterr Stair or stare at.

Stoap Stop.

Stoat/Stoated Hit. As in *If you don't watch your manners I'll stoat you around the ear!*

Stoater/Stoatin Stunningly attractive. As in *She's a real wee stoater* or *She's really stoatin*. Made particularly popular by the late Jack Milroy and Rikki Fulton as *Francie and Josie*.

Stoshus Very drunk.

Swally Swallow. As in *Do you fancy a wee swally?/Would you care for a small libation?*

Swamp donkey An ugly woman.

Swankin Joking. As in *I was only swankin, you're not really a swamp donkey.*

Swatch Look at. As in *Gies a swatch of yer newspaper/Give me a look at your newspaper.*

Swedgers Sweets.

T is for...

Tadz Graffiti.

Tae To. As in *Do you want tae go oot wi me tonight?/Would you like to step out with me this evening?*

Tallyman A money lender.

Tan/Tanned/Tanning To beat someone up or to finish off, usually a quantity of alcohol. As in *He fairly tanned that bottle of whisky*.

Tank/Tanked/Tankin Similar to the above. As in *He gave him a real tankin* or *He really tanked that whisky*.

Tap The top or to borrow from. As in *The tap of the hill* or *Could you tap me £5?* Also *tappa/top of*.

Tarrier A Roman Catholic.

Tate/Tait A small amount. Similar to 'smidgeon'.

Tawkin Talking. As in *Ah'm tawkin tae you!/Listen up - I'm talking to you!*

Tayed Taken or reserved. As in *That table is tayed*.

Teem/Teemin Pour/pouring or an abundance of.

As in *The rain is teemin doon* or *The river is teemin with fish*. Similar to 'hoachin'.

Telt Told. As in *Ah telt you so!/I told you so!*

Ten club A young female Ned. (see 'Ned').

Terr Tear, rip. As in *Terr it up/Tear it up*.

Thur/Thurs Their/Theirs As in *That's thur business/That's their business*.

Tink A poor person or a scruffy person. As in *He looks like a tink in those clothes*.

Tinnies Tin cans.

Toarn Torn, ripped.

Toarn faced Torn faced. Complaining and miserable looking.

Toaty Very small.

Tool A useless person. As in *He's a real tool!*

Toon Town. How Glaswegians fondly refer to their city centre.

Totties Potatoes.

Trackies Tracksuit top and bottoms. A popular everyday item of apparel for many Glaswegians.

Trippen Laughing.

Tube A useless, empty headed person.

Tuppeny wan Tuppeny one. A punch on the nose.

Tyke A mattress.

U is for...

Um I am. As in *Um really enjoying reading this*.

Underblaw/Underblow Under, beneath. As in *I drapped it underblaw the table/I dropped it under the table*.

Ur Are. As in *You ur/You are*.

Urnae Are not. As in *No, you urnae getting a loan frae me/No, you are not getting a loan from me*.

V is for...

Voddy Vodka. A favourite tipple of Glesca ladies when *oot fur a night oan the toon/out for a night in the city centre*, normally mixed with either orange juice or tonic watter (water). As in *I fancy a wee voddy. Easy oan the tonic watter!*

W is for...

Wacky/Whacky Baccy Cannabis or hash.

Wae With.

Wallie close A tenement close (see 'close') considered a bit posh because it boasts ceramic tiles on the walls.

Wallies Teeth.

Wan One.

Wanan One and. As in a passenger may say to the bus driver *Gies a wanan a half* (an adult ticket and a child's ticket) *tae the toon*.

Wanner In one go.

Wean/Weans A child/children.

Wee Small.

Wee Man A fond term for one's young son or a fond greeting to a friend or stranger of small stature. Also see 'Big Man'.

Weech/weeched Throw/threw/thrown. As in *I weeched the stone into the river*.

Weegie Edinburgh term for a Glaswegian.

Wheesht Quiet. As in *Haud yer wheesht!/Be quiet!*

Whit What. As in *Whit are you talking about?*

White scud Cheap and nasty white wine.

White tea Cheap and nasty white wine or cider.

Whitey/Take a Time off work because of illness/sickness.

Wid Would.

Wide-O Untrustworthy or a bit of a conman. As in *Don't get involved with him, he's a real wide-o.*

Widnae Would not.

Wild/Wild wae it Off one's head on strong alcohol.

Windae Window.

Wisnae Was not. As in *It wisnae me, ask emdy!/It wasn't me, ask anyone!*

Wull Will. As in *I wull/I will*.

Wullnae Will not. *As in I wullnae.*

Wur Our. Similar to 'oor'.

X is for...

Xboax X Box. Popular device for playing computer games.

X burd/X man/X wife Former partner.

Xcellently Very good, very well done.

Xcommunicated Thrown out, in disgrace, beyond the pale.

X Files/The Tales of 'beyond this world' experiences of a typical Glaswegian, normally after a night out.

Y is for...

Ya You. As in the expressions of delight *Ya Dancer!* and *Ya Beauty!*

Yer/Yur You're. As in *Yer bum is oot the windae/Your backside is hanging out of the window*, meaning *You have no chance whatsoever*.

Yersel Yourself. As in the common greeting to a

friend whom you may not have met for some time *It's yersel!*

Yon　That. As in *Do you see yon man over there?*

Z is for...

Zebedeed　Under the influence of drugs. Derived from 'Zebedee', a laid-back character from the children's television show *The Magic Roundabout*.

Zingin　Full of energy. Firing on all cylinders or under the influence of drugs.

Zombied　Heavily under the influence of drugs. Also see 'Quality Men'.

Zoomer　A madcap.

ZZZs　Snores induced by deep sleep. Pronounced 'zees' or 'zeds'. As in *He wiz giving it heavy ZZZs last night/He was snoring very loudly.*

MORE GREAT GLASGOW TITLES FROM LANG SYNE

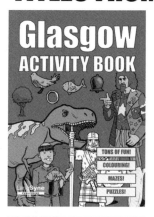

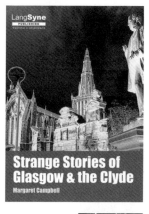

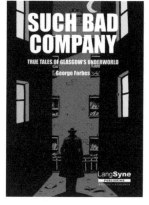